our nuyorican Thing

THE BIRTH OF A SELF-MADE IDENTITY

our nuyorican Thing

THE BIRTH OF A SELF-MADE IDENTITY

A compendium of emails, poetry and
short prose about the Nuyorican experience

by Samuel Diaz Carrion
Introduction by Urayoán Noel
with a Foreword by Clare Ultimo

NUYORICAN WORLD SERIES

NEW YORK
www.2leafpress.org

P.O. Box 4378
Grand Central Station
New York, New York 10163-4378
editor@2leafpress.org
www.2leafpress.org

2LEAF PRESS
is an imprint of the
Intercultural Alliance of Artists & Scholars, Inc. (IAAS),
a NY-based nonprofit 501(c)(3) organization that promotes
multicultural literature and literacy.
www.theiaas.org

Copyright © 2014 by Samuel Diaz Carrion
Cover art and design: Clare Ultimo
Author photo: Vagabond Beaumont
Book design and layout: Gabrielle David

Library of Congress Control Number: 2013953972
ISBN-13: 978-1-940939-07-0 (Paperback)
ISBN-13: 978-1-940939-08-7 (eBook)
BISAC: Poetry / Caribbean & Latin American

10 9 8 7 6 5 4 3 2 1

Published in the United States of America

First Edition | First Printing

2LEAF PRESS trade distribution is handled by University of Chicago Press / Chicago Distribution Center (www.press.uchicago.edu) 773.702.7010. Titles are also available for corporate, premium, and special sales. Please direct inquiries to the UCP Sales Department, 773.702.7248.

The Publisher wishes to thank Vagabond Beaumont for Sam's press photos and wonderful book video. Special thanks to Urayoán Noel for writing a great introduction and lending his name to this project, and to Kevin Tobar Pesántez for editing this groundbreaking collection. Mad love to Carmen Pietri Diaz for everything she does for 2Leaf Press, and more importantly, thanks to Sam for allowing us to present his work.

Dedicatorium

This collection of comments, notes, opinions
("Our Nuyorican Thing") and poems, is dedicated to:

My Father, Ramon C Diaz, who taught me the Word

My Mother, Lucila Carrion Rivera, who taught me Love of the Word

My Wife, Partner, Best Friend and Inspiration,
Carmen M. Pietri who convinced me to put it in print.

To all my Poets, Artists, Musicians and Workers
who Labour to create, as Life does.

CONTENTS

FOREWORD
Sam Diaz, Nuyorican Things and Appreciation from an Italian-American

SAM DIAZ ALWAYS REMINDED ME OF an anthropologist (a Puerto Rican Indiana Jones type with his trademark hat and spectacles too), but instead of fossils and carbon dating, he was quietly studying the trade route of a new language as it moved from one country to another, collecting poetry and stories as the artifacts of the day. He always seemed to be on a quest to reveal the deeper strata hidden beneath appearances. With *Our Nuyorican Thing: The Birth of a Self-Made Identity,* Sam helps us to understand the foundation and true meaning of what it means to be "Nuyorican."

Before I ever met Sam, the term "Nuyorican" was attached to a space, a location where I reawakened a precious part of myself as an artist. In 1993, when I first walked through the door at 236 East Third Street for the Friday Open Mic, I thought I heard a whisper in the room say "this is your home" and I actually laughed out loud nervously at what seemed to be a ridiculous notion. I didn't pay much attention to it afterwards but as I became a Friday night fixture at the Cafe, others would swear to the "fact" they could hear the voices of poets and artists long gone, whispering through the walls of the place; ghosts of the Puerto Rican/Lower East Side/Manhattan variety, you might say. I figured it was just another way that an artistic muse could reach into your head to inspire you. People said it was the secret voice of the "Nuyorican."

If there was a secret voice, it was saying great things to me back then. At this place and with these people, you were encouraged to express whatever you were feeling or thinking and whether the audience heckled you or not, you were still having fun. I regularly wrote poetry at the break between the Slam and the Open Room on Friday nights, and would sign my name in the marble notebook to read this unedited thing in front of a couple of insomniacs at 3:00 a.m. on what came to be known as "the biggest little stage in the world." It was a far cry from corporations, clients, invoices, employees and the headaches that filled my days as Art Director and business owner. It was my personal emancipation.

Five years later this personal emancipation took a surprising turn. After years of avoiding the inevitable—keeping my profession and my poetry as far apart as possible—I brought the Designer/Art Director part of me to the service of the Cafe—putting a public face to their homemade creativity. During my time as their Design Director, I created the Nuyorican Poets Cafe logo and branding, their first press kit, a series of over 50 products for sale online, all kinds of ads and promotion, and an extensive website. I took my devotion to new heights however, when I became deeply involved with their infamous Poetry Slam program (then at its pinnacle under the leadership of Keith Roach) and developed the original Slam publicity, the first *Nuyorican Slam* magazine, and eventually found myself encouraging or comforting National Slam Team members in the wee hours of the morning. Every summer for ten years, I accompanied groups of ambitious and youthful word lovers around the country for

National Poetry Slams and was dubbed "SlamMama" by Mayda Del Valle, our 2001 Grand Slam Champion. It was during this time that I began to work regularly with Sam as well as Carmen Pietri (then the Executive Director), who among other things, were steadfast supporters of Nuyorican Slam. (See *www.verbsonasphalt.com* for more).

Being so deeply absorbed behind-the-scenes didn't make me feel like a Nuyorican though. After so many years of involvement and dedication, I still wasn't sure if I understood the meaning of the word. To complicate matters, ask ten people at any given night at the Cafe what the term meant, and you'd get ten different answers. Then Sam came along in 2001 with a sporadic but illuminating column on the Cafe website called "Our Nuyorican Thing," and I was introduced to an essential perspective. He wrote poetically about the "discovery of new lands," the "interaction between groups, language and identity" and I began to recognize the true significance of the word. "Our Nuyorican Thing" was my initiation to the ingenuity of the Nuyorican attitude, which went far beyond being a Puerto Rican from New York City.

As I witnessed the Cafe audiences that packed the house every week, like gatherings of a poetic United Nations in constantly surprising combinations, I began to see what Sam was talking about. Nuyorican was the "self-made identity" inherent in all of us. We are all somehow combined and displaced, far from home and forced to invent the rules along the way. At the root of it all, "Nuyorican" is a description of originality and artistic imagination. And back in the day, the Nuyorican Poets Cafe was New York's living metaphor of urban creativity. Now that *Our Nuyorican Thing: The Birth of a Self-Made Identity* has become this wonderful book, everyone gets a chance to enjoy a first-hand account of this amazing cultural revolution.

So maybe Puerto Ricans adopted the term "Nuyorican" because they were tired of being asked to shut up and sit down. Maybe they were just less fearful of American opinion than my Italian grandfathers were, but I was tired of being silent too, and these poetic, rebellious Puerto Ricans from the Lower East Side gave artists from everywhere the permission and encouragement to speak up. In the end, it never really mattered what country the words came from. In transcending apparent labels and definitions, Nuyorican could belong to everyone—and it did—a double edged sword but the inevitable result of an incredible cultural experiment.

Sam, a genuine New York Puerto Rican, secret anthropologist of the Lower East Side, poet, writer and artist, represents the true Nuyorican. Knowing him gave me a heartfelt sense that creativity was inclusive and everyone had feelings that were important, no matter what language they spoke. Lucky for us that Sam had the good sense to write down what he was discovering back then, so that he could share the real meaning of Nuyorican with creative souls everywhere.

Despite the fact that the Nuyorican Poets Cafe I discovered long ago is a memory now, and much of its enormous spirit darkened by the politics of our day, it will always be the place where I became a poet again, where I would finally come to see that even an Italian girl from Brooklyn had Nuyorican roots. I was fortunate to have experienced it when it was the "freshest" as Lois Griffith would say. Thank you Sam for keeping it real. Thank you for showing me that this spirit still lives within all those who shared its beginnings. I know how corny it sounds—places come and go but the soul of what is truly "Nuyorican" is written on my heart in indelible ink.

...Ustedes saben quienes son, mis amores. ◀

—Clare Ultimo
February 2014

PREFACE
Before the Beginning

I WAS ASSOCIATED WITH friends, artists, and activists of the Nuyorican Arts Movement of the early 1970s and later read, performed and attended events at the East 6th Street Nuyorican Poets Cafe until it moved to East 3rd Street. After this, I took a long break from the arts to address community issues in my neighborhood in the Bronx. In the late 1990s I was asked to help out at the Cafe, first as an office services consultant and then as an employee. In the Spring of 2001 I began responding to email inquiries by many of the Nuyorican Poets Cafe online members as well as inquiries by visitors and local community residents. Some inquiries were related to Cafe events and day-to-day operations, but many were more generalized as to the origin, purpose and even the meaning of the Cafe's name, "Nuyorican," which required some thought in responding. I decided to explain as much as possible and combine replies to various questions in a series of emails.

The Director, Carmen M. Pietri-Diaz, suggested that before sending out the replies, they should be reviewed by Cafe staff. Clare Ultimo, the Cafe's Web Designer/Administrator, suggested that I post the correspondence on the Cafe's website as a separate page. The Board and the Director agreed, and I named it "Our Nuyorican Thing." As time went on, this correspondence turned into a series of "mini-essays" with much of it centered on Nuyorican identity. These entries resonated with members and patrons of The Nuyorican Poets Cafe, and proved to be an engaging blog series. I began posting my email responses in 2001, and wrote the last installment in April 2004.

This book, *Our Nuyorican Thing, The Birth Of A Self-Made Identity,* is a compilation of some of those commentaries, including some of my poems that were performed at Cafe events relating to "Our Nuyorican Thing." For example, the first poem, "A Prayer for The Living," was read at the Cafe in December 2001, and became the basis for the Annual Proclamation of a Planetary Day of Peace on January 1st.

My relationship with the Cafe goes back to its inception. I was there when a small group of poets, writers and activists like Miguel Algarin, Miguel Piñero, Bimbo Rivas, Pedro Pietri, Lucky Cienfuegos, Jesús Papoleto Meléndez, Sandra Maria Esteves and others came together to create a space to meet and perform. The Cafe was founded during the height of the Nuyorican Arts Movement in the early 1970s. It was a cultural and intellectual movement that validated and documented the Puerto Rican experience in the United States, particularly for poor and working-class people who suffered from marginalization, ostracism and discrimination.

Since I was born in New York and lived in Puerto Rico for about 25 years, my identity was always questioned. When Algarin and Piñero used "Nuyorican" to name the Cafe and insisted on making the term theirs (not without arguments, deliberations and finally acceptance), it was this very process of establishing identity that drove me and many of my friends in the Nuyorican

Arts Movement to question our identity. In time, it moved from an ethnic/cultural distinction to a more inclusive artistic identity. It was self-made, proclaimed and asserted.

The term, "Nuyorican" is not new, it has been in use since at least 1964 in a few places in Puerto Rico, and was applied retroactively to persons that fit the description to previous generations. Over time, its meaning has changed and shifted from a derogatory term by native Puerto Ricans when describing someone of Puerto Rican ancestry born and/or raised in the ethnic enclaves of New York City and various urban centers throughout the U.S. (where migrant workers from the island settled), to becoming a positive term of cultural recognition and acceptance. While many of my fellow Puerto Ricans were born and raised in New York, they too experienced the cultural duality of the mainland and the island. Certainly, this new term, "Nuyorican" provided an identity they were proud to be associated with.

The Cafe initially represented a beautiful synergy of Nuyorican and African American spirits that celebrated life. By the mid-1990s when performance poetry and slam had gained considerable momentum, the Cafe had come to embody the essence of an independent, organically grown multicultural arts expression in New York City.

Books like *Nuyorican Poetry: An Anthology of Puerto Rican Words and Feelings* (1975) edited by Algarin and Miguel Piñero, and *Aloud: Voices from the Nuyorican Poets Cafe* (1994) edited by Miguel Algarin and Bob Holman helped drive this point home. In fact, many began to believe that the term "Nuyorican" had grown to embrace this new artistic way of thinking. These ideas were brewing by the time I began working at The Nuyorican Cafe and was writing for the "Our Nuyorican Thing" web page.

"Our Nuyorican Thing" grew into the birth of a self-made identity that celebrated the confluence of political activism, cultural ingenuity and artistic expression of a Nuyorican culture that was now open to everyone. Besides becoming culturally inclusive, Nuyorican is no longer geographically bound — Puerto Ricans can be found everywhere throughout the contiguous United States—yet many identify themselves as "Nuyorican." While some would say Nuyorican has definitely become "our thing," the term itself remains a controversial topic among Puerto Ricans on both the island and the mainland. So even though this collection of commentaries is almost ten years old, many of the issues I raised then remain relevant today.

As much as the origin of the Nuyorican identity was started by children playing, artists sharing and communities interacting, its growth, development and establishment will continue to evolve. It can be said that the definition of who we are is in essence a work of art in progress, and perhaps therein lays the key to the future of this, *Our Nuyorican Thing*. I hope readers will enjoy this journey as much as I did writing about it. ◄

—Samuel Diaz Carrion
Bronx, New York
In the Service of Poetry, Art and Community

INTRODUCTION
Finding Our Nuyoricaness in
Our Nuyorican Thing

OUR NUYORICAN THING is essential reading for anyone interested in this groundbreaking yet still misunderstood movement. As poet, writer, chemist, and community worker Samuel Diaz Carrion reminds us, this Nuyorican thing was and is about many things, including poetry, music, art, activism, language, and community. Diaz Carrion should know: he was there at the inception of the Nuyorican Poets Cafe, the New Rican Village, and other legendary venues and initiatives, and this book builds on short pieces he wrote as blog entries for the Nuyorican Poets Cafe website during the early to mid-2000s.

With its mix of poetry and cultural commentary, this book is itself an extension of the Nuyorican tradition, which blurred the boundaries between creative expression and cultural mobilization. Correctly and crucially, Diaz Carrion locates Nuyorican identity beyond mere cultural affirmation (flag waving, representing) and also in the unrepresentable, in the complexities and contradictions of an "Alien Nation / far flung / across TIME, SPACE / and Gravitation." On the one hand, *Our Nuyorican Thing* is about a shift in perception: like New Rican Village-founder Eddie Figueroa, Diaz Carrion urges us to look inwards and re-create ourselves, pledging "allegiance to the Spirit Republic / and the creativity for which it stands." Similarly, like Pedro Pietri, Diaz Carrion invites us to claim a strategic in/visibility, and to listen to the silence in our social voice as a way to cut through the static of empire: "a silence that elicits a response, a silence that questions, a silence that manages to overwhelm the soul."

On the other hand, this is a book of dispatches, attuned to histories plural, that addresses and sheds light on some tricky yet fundamental issues: the history of the term Nuyorican, the politics and poetics of Spanglish, the sociocultural role of poetry readings and performances, the tensions between art and community (and inside and outside), the complicated relationship between Nuyorican and island Puerto Rican art and culture, and the changing terms of community in the post-9/11 techno-global moment.

Our Nuyorican Thing is also important because it documents a period of transition (the post-millennium) characterized by the gentrification of the Lower East Side and the commodification of Nuyorican slam poetry, and in fact Diaz Carrion considers Nuyorican art, identity, and community history in the context of the mass media spectacles of the *Piñero* biopic (2001) and the *Def Poetry Jam on Broadway* show (2002-03). In this context, Diaz Carrion's refrain "You too are a Nuyorican" is as hopeful and poignant as it is provocative, insisting on a self-made creative community while blogging from the belly of the new, neoliberal New York.

Although the book calls itself a "compendium of emails, poetry and short prose about the Nuyorican experience," I prefer to think of it as a collection of essays in Montaigne's original sense of the term: as attempts, say, to explore this Nuyorican thing by bringing into (and sometimes strategically out of) focus. This mode of personal-social exploration is of course what

Nuyorican poets have been doing for half a century now. *Our Nuyorican Thing* helps frame this history, but it also reminds us of our fundamental no-thingness, of our bodies in their uneasy becoming, in and out of breath. Diaz Carrion maps this Nuyorican thing partly by foregrounding the dialectics in the dialects, the paradoxes of identity. ◄

—Urayoán Noel
New York University, author of
In Visible Movement: Nuyorican Poetry from the Sixties to Slam

I.
Prelude

FOR US AT THE CAFE it's obvious that the events of September 11th are not over as each day brings in more news that proves we are under attack. Having grieved the demise of so many, comforted the afflicted, consoled the survivors, and thanked the helpful hands of so many unknown heroes, in the aftermath we are faced with physical and mental health afflictions, the loss of jobs and the curtailment of revenue, our political process suspended (the cancellation of our primaries looming in the air), cancelled sports games (where it looks like we actually might make it to, the World Series PLEASE!), and even questioning our spiritual and religious beliefs (was this really done in the name of some God?).

A call for a return to normalcy may seem a bit too much to ask for as we walk into what appears to be wartime, but there is still some comfort knowing we're somehow safe. How is it that we're all part of a species that can express itself creatively, yet is capable of creating such horrors? But all is not lost. It is my privilege, while I am preparing this notice, to hear artists rehearsing and practicing, poets prepping and musicians tuning up to get ready for the next show. I want to thank them for helping me keep the faith (so tested these past couple of days) by continuing to go forward.

Since September 11th, I have received notices from many cultural and artist groups around the country wishing us well as they come together to do what comes naturally to them: Working for Peace. I will keep you updated as space allows. ◄

[Oct. 18, 2001, emailed]

2.
Words

THERE IS HEALING IN THE WORD. We also know that words can also hurt, as any kid will tell you. Even with the best intentions, we sometimes hurt people by the words we choose, and sometimes people are hurt by what they choose to hear. And when you put it all down on paper, it remains forever immortalized.

At the Cafe, we sometimes walk on the jagged edge of perception. We don't censor the expression of art, and we cannot, dare not, control how the audience will react. I'd like to think that the artists here at the Cafe are serving some higher purpose, and I hope, pray and keep my fingers crossed that the art somehow shines through to entertain, heal wounds, and bridge the gap of our human experiences in such a way that helps us to grow. And if art doesn't always reach this higher purpose, at least we should have a good time trying. We should never stop trying!

Perhaps it's a sign of the times, but we seem much more aware, sensitive and reactive since September 11th and I think many of us, including myself, wonder if our reflexes are as reliable as they used to be. I think we're second-guessing ourselves, questioning how to react to things we never thought about. How else should we react? I think what might help is if we recommit ourselves in search of all that is good, peaceful and creative within us, and learn how to see it in each other.

Seek peace, seek love, seek justice, seek truth and don't just sit there reading about it: Go out and work for it. Go out and find it! And if you can't find it, make it happen!◄

[Oct 25, 2001, emailed]

3.
Words & Poetry, War & Peace!

HOW'S THAT FOR SCARY? Words, poetry and peace go hand-in-hand in opposition to war. First of all, since the Cafe was founded on poetry, art and community, artists come here to express their creative impulses by extending, stretching, and playing with the meaning of words to convey art, images and ideas that serve to enrich the audience. All of these actions amount to peace.

The funny thing about war is that it has become an acceptable mode of behavior in our society. It even has legislated procedures and rules of engagement. The difference between war and peace is that people think that peace is just the absence of war, when nothing could be further from the truth. What's strange is that peace doesn't have the same rules of engagement as war. This is why I believe that peace should have its own legislated procedures and rules of engagement with clear objectives, and should be defined and declared.

So how about something real tangible for starters: Let's have a Planetary Day of Peace. Twenty-four hours in which no human sheds human blood. How about the first day of the year, sounds feasible? It's simple and straightforward. Perhaps if we can get through one day of peace, that day will become two or three, or a week or more. Maybe we can last with several months of peace. Who knows? Anything is possible!

Allow me, on behalf of the Cafe, and for all the poets and artists everywhere, by the powers and authority vested in me by my Word as a Poet, to hereby proclaim January 1st of each year as Planetary Day of Peace: "Let no human shed human blood for one day."

Join me on December 1st at the Nuyorican Poets Cafe when I share my poem, "A Prayer for The Living," that has been read at various venues around town, most recently at the People's Cafe at their Poets for Peace reading last week. And it should be noted that there are many Poets for Peace events being offered here and there. I will keep you posted. ◄

[Oct. 28, 2001]

A Prayer for The Living

A Prayer for the living
must I say
perhaps to appease
the whispers of the wind
carries far the lightest thought
but who will know
of us and all our misdeeds
we travel far
and close die
and long after our remains
have as ruins gone
will You remember us
today
when all is gone
now
when all is lost
will You a candle light
to the memory
of our bleak existence
and lofty dreams
never quite achieving
a total waste of time
much less a small measure
of some self worth

Bound by chains cast
we wish to redo the past
never quite sure
which was the step
that lost us from ourselves
as we redo our own
peculiar perception of the moment
it leaves before

it gets here
and we ask is it real
or the memory of your existence
somewhere but on earth
or maybe some lost place

and perhaps the passage
in between, lays claim
to some justification
to our questions
as we ask You
for another day
not knowing what price to pay
or must we guess
depending on the size of the tip
but we never see the rest

And I
utter a prayer
for the living
a request for peace
but not the one that is to be read
on our obituary in space
"I don't want to rest in peace"
and all I ask if for one day
before I can no longer ask

Let no human
shed human blood
for one day

and if you think
it superstitious of me to ask
have you got

anything to ask for
at all or at least

and if you think
it grievous of me to tempt
fate for speaking in haste
what have you got
that's better than that

So do not interrupt
this prayer for you
and please don't interpret
what I mean
and please don't explain
what is wrong
with a prayer
for the living
spoken by all the children dead
a request for peace
for a race that knows it not
though somewhere
in our ancient
collective memory
perhaps there once was
and if such a garden exists
please show it not to me
not while there is a chance
that by mistake
we should fail
by one or even two
and that is too many

And if it brings tears
to your weary eyes

you might as well
go cry in the rain
and mutter under your breath
a simple prayer for the living

And if you think
it evil of me to ask
for the impossible
and what is not meant to be
then punish me
by letting it be
I'm sorry I'm sorry
I didn't ask it before
but I wasn't sure
what I wanted to ask
I see my mistake
and I'll gladly apologize
but please
don't misjudge until I see it
or know that no one will

I will repeat
a gentle litany
a prayer for the living
and perhaps
you too will whisper it
at night
in the middle of your dreams
when anything is possible

Let no human
shed human blood
for one day

I tell You
I will gladly pay
the last penny and interest too
and don't laugh
at the staggering debt
of a pause in time
in the story of our race

it's just a moment
nothing more
it's just a dream
nothing more
it's words on sand
voices to the wind

And excuse me if
I continue to continue
this silent litany
to justify my existence
and perhaps to gain
a new perspective
on the length
of the measure of our days
and why it continues
long after
you've run
out of excuses or alibis
but for the curious
persistence of this will
to live
and to not know why
and it gets to be sad
when you've forgotten
the length of this sentence
and no reprieve

in view
of the facts of the case
pretending not to care
it does have a bearing
though it goes
'round 'n 'round
the mirages shift
though images persist
and I ask
"till when, till when"
must I say
a prayer for the living
and keep silence
for the dead

Must I add
the grains of sand
that mark
the silent passage
of our hopeless trek
will not sands
cry to the wind
will not the soil
be drenched in blood
add another
drop of blood
to the ocean roar
add another sigh
to the sounds of the night
when all I ask is
"till when, till when"
and don't lose track
of the times we must say
a prayer for the living:

Let no human
shed human blood
for one day

How long must we bare
the center of our souls
to the daily judgment
that we wish upon ourselves
and don't bother
to agree with me
on this one
it doesn't matter
that I'm right
or left behind
for surely someone
must count the times
a prayer for the living
we must cry
or to wait for an answer
or the silence instead
to write our story
a tale of caution
for someone else
and perhaps to
provide a reason why
a prayer for the living
I must say

And I will not
be silenced again
nor will I
keep it to myself
and when you're done
with this universe
don't bother to interpret

what I say
or translate
what I mean

And remember
to remember
this prayer for the living
whispered by who died in pain
caused or given by a human being

Let no human
shed human blood
for one day

And if we fail the test
I won't mind
taking it again
again and again
until we get it right
and not just close enough
it is not enough
although I'm sure
you'll enjoy whatever you get
I will not rest
until a prayer
for the living is said

But will You wait
and stay the sword
from judgment day
for this one favor
even though it is too much
to barter or pay for
I won't mind begging at all
just once and nothing more

I want to read about it
in the front page
this prayer for the living
for the universe to know

And I promise
cross my heart and hope to die
I will never ask again
may I be punished
to never die if I lie
won't you please join me
at the stroke of mid-night
or my heart
on the first day of the year
marked at ground-time zero
may I please hear
a cry for peace
a requiem to life
a prayer for the living

Let no human
shed human blood
for one day

Please don't think I'm crazy
or even blasphemous
I don't even want to be famous
I just want a day of peace
on a planet in space
that has seen very little of it
and too much death
for this violent race
that has been too much of it
and not enough time
to count

the number of stars
the number of grains
or how many children have died
while we looked away
and I'll be on my way

And please don't hate me
for saying out loud
in the middle of the day
what I wish for
in the still of the night
just because I can not
ignore the screams
borne on the wind
or shut out the whimpers
it does not mean
I am not human
It's not too much
to ask for
though maybe a lot
to wait or hope for
but it's not just
for my enjoyment
that I wish
we would stop
and though I do not
understand why,
somewhere in the distant
event horizon
of our story in space
lies the reason
for our fall from grace
and why we keep
distance from ourselves

A prayer for the living
must I say
to keep the darkness in its place
to shed some light
on our behalf
to understand
the clues hid herein
and the message thereof
our story unfolds
true to course
regardless of your choice
and though there is
no end in sight
the sentence remains
to cry again and again
a prayer for the living
till you say when

Let no human
shed human blood
for one day

And if it seems
that I am
endlessly repeating
these words
in flesh engraved
waiting for a sign
to tell me why
or till when
must I say
a prayer for the living
it's only that
I just want to see
a prayer for the living

come true
if only but once

Let no human
shed human blood
for one day

Pledge of Allegiance

I pledge allegiance
to Poetry and words written or not
I pledge allegiance
to the Galactocosmic Ordum Dominis
I pledge allegiance
to life wherever it be
I pledge allegiance
to planet earth and all within
I pledge allegiance to the Spirit Republic
and the creativity for which it stands
one life universal in all the shapes and forms
it wishes to reveal itself or not
indivisible, eternal and unique
in all of its voices

I pledge allegiance
to all and anything that seeks life
that nurtures, protects and propagates
that expresses, enjoys and celebrates
life

I pledge allegiance
to myself and to you
for all of eternity and a day

4.
The Cafe

Age: No age limits other than in compliance with NY State and City laws pertaining to alcoholic beverages

Cover Charge: Entry fees [and/or suggested donations] per event

Attire: Wear something (I'm kidding, no I'm not), just proper, appropriate.

WE'RE ON A MISSION. We're attempting to define the term "Nuyorican" (not what, but who...). Do you have any ideas on how to define Nuyorican? When you do, please take into account its root origin pertains to Puerto Ricans from New York. I first heard the term back in 1965 in Puerto Rico. It was given by one local to another in reference to a mutual friend, in a slightly patronizing way. When did you first hear the term? Please share. ◄

[Nov. 8, 2001, emailed (portion)]

5.
Definitions: Nuyoricans

WE HAVE EMBARKED ON THE PROCESS of defining who we are as Nuyoricans. When I first heard the term in 1965, it was a descriptive label applied by someone else. The first time I heard someone call himself a Nuyorican was in 1967 and he wasn't even from New York, he was from Chicago. Since I've been getting responses from many of you indicating some personal experiences and perspectives about the term "Nuyorican," I thought it would be a great idea to talk about this label, which continues to change and grow.

When a poet from Israel claims to be a Nuyorican poet, and I happen to agree, one friend reminds me that there was once a darker label applied to us, while another reminds me how fluid labels are, especially the ones we apply to ourselves. It's interesting that the Israeli, who lives on the other side of the world lays claim to this label, "Nuyorican." While Miguel Algarin, Lucky, Mikey, Pedro Petri, Papoleto and many others reclaimed this term, it has recently evolved from a descriptive label of a specific cultural-artistic-ethnic hybrid to include anyone who chooses to identify with this process.

I'm fascinated how the term Nuyorican has evolved and grown. I think the idea of Nuyorican began organically, probably as simple as children using slang terms derived from their native tongues, into something that we now call "Spanglish" (topic for another time), with different cultures experiencing similar trends around the country and the world. We're all strangers, but we're not. Because when we meet, we speak the same lingo and we connect, like children playing with words. ◄

[Nov. 2001]

6.
Who/What/Labels

IT'S OBVIOUS THAT AS WE ANALYZE the meaning of the term, "Nuyorican," there's more to it that meets the eye, so to speak. The Nuyorican Poets Cafe founder, Miguel Algarin, adopted a term that was used in Puerto Rico as a condescending and derogatory term for those children of Puerto Rican emigrants who were raised in the U.S. (at that time, mostly in New York, Chicago and New Jersey). This generation of "Nuyoricans" spoke with an accented Spanish, created Spanish terms (known as "Spanglish"), adopted American mannerisms and cultural likes and dislikes (especially music), and had a more metropolitan perspective about themselves and the world around them. They even walked differently!

I think the questions I want to explore are: How does art address the idea of identity? How do artists working today reveal and question commonly held assumptions about stereotypes, self-awareness, and what does it mean to be an artist?

Cultural practices, especially the purposeful making of things, embody our values and, I would argue, are the basis of the good mental health of a society. These practices help contribute to an individual and collective sense of identity, citizenship and community. Art is a self-affirming activity, which helps us to interpret, think about, add to or challenge our cultural life.

Here are some questions we should ask ourselves in this exploration of identity and self:

> What are you?
> Who are you?
> Are you a poet, because you call yourself a poet, or someone else calls you poet
> Do you use labels to be included or excluded?

Over the course of our 5,000 plus years of recorded history, humans, in an attempt to "know thyself" have used terms to describe "us" versus "them." I believe the distinction was made, not only to identify the differences between different cultures and languages, but it's also used as a means to conquer, enslave and go to war.

That's why I've grown to appreciate the lost world of human values embodied in cultural practices, before profit was all. We should work together to help children to read so they can learn their cultural roots. Why? This supports the retention of a strong identity in the face of unstoppable forces at the gate.

The dictionary defines identity as:

> "the state or fact of remaining the same one or ones, as under varying aspects or conditions. The condition of being oneself or itself and not another."

Developing a personal identity is crucial in the development of human beings. Knowing who you are, what you believe, how you stand in trials and triumphs, why you make certain choices, are all established through experience and exposure. All these factors are impacted by peers and popular media. It goes beyond being identified as "Nuyorican." The true question is: "Do you know who you are?" When you're able to figure that out, it's only then when you'll gain the courage to reach deep within yourself to discover your own true identity. ◄

[Nov. 2001]

7.
Originals

THE GENERATION THAT WAS CONFRONTED with a derogatory label proclaimed it, ran with it and had fun: Nuyorican!!! And in so doing, they started a new term slightly divorced from its initial meaning, not quite sure what it was, now knowing what it wasn't, all the while attracting an urban mix of children into this strange quest for identity.

Initially, the term was used in the neighborhood and amongst ourselves. It was "our thing," but gradually in time it broke barriers and was adopted into the American lexicon. Like a "sancocho" mix (thick soup with meats, Caribbean condiments, spices, starchy vegetables, salsa, and the kitchen sink), Nuyorican gave a new "flava" to this old town and even beyond.

In time, a new trend in identity has been the loose adoption of interchangeable labels. From Poet to Slammer to Hip-Hop to Spoken Word; from Puerto Rican to Nuyorican through Latino by way of Hispanic, this birth of planetary labels have appeared organically, without borders or turf. Yet despite this trend, most of the planet is still embroiled in labeling people with an "us" versus "them" mentality that's meant to keep us apart rather than coming together.

But I also want to point out that there is no one definition of "Nuyorican." Having taken on these fluid self-anointed labels, we live in a pluralistic polyglot society that expresses itself in different languages. If we remain true to our nature, we simply continue to change, adapt, adopt and grow, bridging ourselves to other cultures along the way.

You too are a Nuyorican. *Welcome Home.* ◄

[Dec. 6, 2001]

It's About

it's about an old story
    without end & no moral within
    told in languages long dead,
    inscribed in genotypic memories,
    inherited by the wind

it's about an end at the edge
    of a desert without borders,
    hollow sounds drifting on sand
    sketching upon the surface of time:
    a story that goes on and on

it's about grains of sand
    & the words written thereon
    for no one to read or remember
    how it began or why it ends
    in questions wailing in the wind

it's about words without meaning
    & the purpose therein
    to recall the ancient question why
    in blood we leave our tracks
    & in graves our dreams

it's about beginnings
    and following through
    in the multiple implied choices
    set upon our paths
    & all the roads we cross

it's about seeking patterns
    in our rambling random numbers
    & the stories we choose to hear

when no one is near
to see the insights that blind us

it's about questions and answers
and the silences
in between the voices you hear
when you thought you understood
what we were talking about

it's about coming and not going,
living & not dying, sleeping
and not dreaming impossible dreams
that require you to be awake
for your screams to be heard

it's about poems spoken to the wind,
written on sand
in all the languages we use
to obscure all we want to say
& clarify what we choose to hide.

it's about a language
now dead and soon forgot
the mysteries of our past
& the legend of a future
that comes and never gets here

it's about terrors of the mind
borne naked at noon,
all our deeds seen in broad daylite
silent witnesses for our trials
and silence our due sentence

it's about crying in relief
when the sun comes up

to laugh in the face of death
as it gravely stares
while you step six feet under

it's about love unrequited
& the passions withheld
the empty affairs of the mind
the mindless compulsion of life
bearing witness to itself

it's about trying always trying,
never stopping
& in all of its permutations
life seeks to conquer entropy
dissipating, ever extending.

it's about walking without roads,
ever wandering never getting there
or knowing it or
staying here long enough to see
all the trails about

it's about traveling without a map
& not getting lost
knowing not your destination
or the reason why not
or the difference if there is any

it's about staring at empty pages
and or blank walls
that compel you to draw the design
of your ignorant choice
or suffer the consequences

it's about hoping you're wrong
    but you're not
    and you know it
    in the psychopathic certainty
    of the consensus
    of the voices in your mind

it's about knowing but not why
    without reason or rhyme
    you spend your life
    a second at a time
    to the inevitable conclusion of it all

it's about breathing in order to live
    or living in order to dream
    or dreaming without an order in mind
    in the entropic disorder
    of your vision spent

it's about not knowing why
    but doing despite
    all the reasons not to
    that compel you to fill
    a blank page with sounds
    upon the wind into a poem

it's about a poem that
    repeats itself in
    an endless succession of words
    striving to underline a purpose
    to all your deeds & life

Eat Rocks

[poem for Pedro based on his work in progress for a play]

Eat rocks
in the middle of the day
and have some sand for dessert
wash it down with oil
and put on black lipstick
and smile with the hole
south of your nose
for all is well now
and then
eat rocks

Eat rocks
as you walk the graveyard shift
in second gear ready for more
where there is no more
just tracks on dirt veins
to call out your name
when you can't hear
the facts of the matter
not that you care
why you now
Eat rocks

Eat rocks
when you smile at the cost
of your demise without interest,
down-payments, excuses or alibis
for a dark day yet to come
and save your stories, songs and poems
for a rainy day
and while you dream
eat rocks

Eat rocks
as you digest the nuggets
that always shine late at night
and wake up in the morning
and pretend you are not asleep
while you dream movie scripts
to tell you what comes next
in case you have forgot
remember to
eat rocks

Eat rocks
as you grind your teeth
in stolid determination
against the rising tide of the sea
and wake me when it's over
to tell me the story of your choice
regardless of the outcome
beginning or end
eat rocks

Eat rocks
put on a dress with no destination
but to seduce you with your self
as you contemplate
your next brilliant word or silence
screaming at the red full moon
in the middle of a burning desert
and tell me to get out of your way
eat rocks

Eat rocks
savor all that is left
and remains deep underground
till you know not who you were

which way you came
or how much you will pay
to stay another day
to find out what's the word
you missed the most
eat rocks

Eat rocks
as you work out your debt
in a forever monthly charge
to keep you lean and mean
to make it seem all worthwhile
while you run
to your next chosen task
in the guise of a vision
that is fit for us all
and don't forget to
eat rocks

Happy Birthday, Miguel

It was a good day
for a bright fall
to take a leap
    into the unknown
    a week without end
    a month to see
    a year I would
    not soon forget

Still too early to tell
I decided to not go
    (into the day)
to a date
with a test
for a job
I sorely needed
but did not want

And I would have been
closer to the place
where a party
would happen
later "that" day
where I would say
"Happy Birthday"

But I did not attend
the party that did not happen

And now,
    so many years later
all I can say is
"Happy Birthday"
and stay home

8.
Comments

DURING THE PAST FEW UPDATES I have been discussing who and what is "Nuyorican." But now a technical pause for some disclaimers:

1. The comments, views and opinions contained in these updates are not to be taken as Nuyorican Poets Cafe (NPC) policy or views. They are mine, and mine alone.

2. Events taking place at the NPC are the sole responsibility of the producers of the event. Statements, opinions, performances at such events should not be considered the views of the NPC.

3. The NPC provides a space, a floor, a forum to the free expression of art in its many forms. The NPC does not censor the content or the performance of art, nor does it censor the reaction of the audience. ◄

[Dec. 13, 2001, emailed]

9.
Piñero, the Film

I WOULD LIKE TO SHARE WITH YOU some of my comments on the film, *Piñero* (February 14th National Release, December 14th, opens in NY, UA Union Square).

This is not a review. I am neither a critic nor a reviewer. The film is the work of Leon Ichaso, the producers, financial backers, actors and Miramax. The Nuyorican Poets Cafe as an entity had nothing to do with the film. It did not approve or disapprove the film; scripts were not submitted to the Cafe, nor was there any reason to do so. The Cafe gave permission to use its name and its location. Although certain individuals associated with the Cafe were contracted for consultation and to make an appearance in the film, they were not representing the Nuyorican Poets Cafe as an entity.

A post-screening event that took place at the Cafe was a Miramax sponsored event for their own corporate purposes. I was pleased that they chose to do it at the Cafe, however we were led to believe that it was an open affair. It was not. Or as Mikey would have said: "they gave me a party, and I wasn't invited."

We all have our views on what constitutes art, film, history, poetry, etc., and as a Nuyorican, I have my own personal memories of the events portrayed in a film about one of ours. I went to see the film with many misgivings and very low expectations. The misgivings were confirmed, my expectations were proven wrong. My misgivings centered on whether the film would attempt to sell itself as a documentary, which it didn't, but it still gave the impression that it was, which it was not. My expectations were centered on having to sit through another American "Latino" film, but it turned out I was wrong. It actually is an artistic film about a poet that happens to be a Nuyorican. I am not one easily moved, but for me there was closure in the final moments, above and beyond all the misrepresentations, inaccuracies, and artistic liberties taken with the life and times of Mikey; a promise made, and a promise kept. His ashes are where they belong, where he wanted them: his Loisaida, and all over.

You too are a Nuyorican. *Welcome Home.* ◄

[Dec. 13, 2001]

10.
Origins: Imagine

IMAGINE HUNDREDS OF KIDS leaving a little island in the Caribe to live in a new country with their family. At about the same time, hundreds of Puerto Rican kids are born and raised in the U.S. (mostly New York, New Jersey, Pennsylvania and Illinois), who really don't know, care or realize the many reasons why their elders made the move to the mainland. These children's paths cross. Imagine when they meet up with each other and start talking and find out they don't completely understand each other. Imagine that. So they do what children do: they play and make up words as they go along. In the process, a strange mix of words from different customs, mores and traditions blend into a new lingo; a loose amalgamation of Spanish sounding English words, English sounding Spanish terms, mixed in with some made-up words somehow makes sense while the older generation looks on perplexed.

What are they saying? But the laughter is too contagious the tears too real—*Rufo* = roof, *Marketa* = market place—and soon this new lingo catches on. "Spanglish" is the term we use for it now, but it existed long before Nuyorican came into our radar. And so I credit the children, who managed to create a language that helped create a label: Nuyorican.

When these children grow up, some of them become poets, writers, playwrights, musicians, dancers and artists. They put the words from their youth to paper, music and canvas, and in doing so they preserve the language in such a way that it becomes part of our culture. Cervantes did it in Spain. Dante did it in Italy. Shakespeare did it England. (No they didn't do it alone, their generation was part of the play.)

And the Nuyoricans have done this: Pedro Pietri, Miguel Algarin and so many others have taken terms and phrases from their youth and brought it into the mainstream through art. And before you get the impression that this is a New York thing; be assured that it continues to happen all over, from California to the Midwest, from the Great Lakes down to the Gulf, from Florida and Louisiana all throughout the South. Children will be children, and some of those children will grow up to become poets and artists.

And so to all the children, and poets, artists and musicians who remain children, I wish you Love. I wish you lots and lots of Fun. And I wish upon you everlasting Peace (although I would settle for one Planetary Day of Peace). ◄

[Dec. 20, 2001]

II.
Nuyoricans: Types/Tipos

IN TALKING ABOUT THE MEANING OF NUYORICAN, it occurred to me that there are different categories of Nuyoricans, and below is a breakdown as I see it:

1. *The Ethnic Nuyorican.* This is Puerto Rican children born on the island and growing up in an American urban metropolis whose family maintains strong ties to the island. Their search for identity is continuous and is often further impaired because of dynamic opposing currents: still dreaming of belonging, still struggling with these schizophrenic pulls from two cultures, two languages, two islands (New York and Puerto Rico), and no homeland. Without the backup of a nuclear "familia" that has dispersed to the suburbs and away from the mean streets of El Barrio, they are always searching for validation and identity. This idea is constantly being reborn, with each new Rican that arrives, with each Nuyorican that leaves. Talking and dreaming in two tongues.

2. *The Bridge Nuyorican.* Puerto Rican children who are born on the mainland and do not have immediate ties to the island, with many of them no longer bound by traditional urban enclaves. They live everywhere, from the East Coast to the West Coast, from the North to the deep South, yet they still identify themselves as "Nuyorican." Theirs is a story spoken in tongues that is bicultural and bilingual, while they deal with their identity in a lingo that resonates in a shared heritage. They are confident and curious about others around them; willing to dance to a new synthesized language that so readily lends itself to poetry and the arts.

3. *The Nuyorican Artist.* Since the founding of the Nuyorican Poets Cafe by Miguel Algarin (first in his apartment, then on East 6th Street, finally on East 3rd Street), the Cafe has remained a forum for free expression of the arts in all its forms. As such, the term of Nuyorican took on a creative, artistic and highly contagious meaning: Art! Here was a place for the artistic side of us, where different art forms run into each other, play with each other and new forms of expression that attracted people from different cultural backgrounds. They too adopted the term Nuyorican, and we Nuyoricans adopted them into our family of poets, musicians, actors, writers and visual artists. We belong to them as much as they belong to us.

Over the years many people have performed and shared their art at the Nuyorican Poets Cafe and have invariably become part of our family, "la familia." It's the birth of a planetary tribe, without borders. Once a Nuyorican, you are home anywhere you go.

You too are a Nuyorican. *Welcome Home.* ◀

[Jan. 2002]

12.
Spanglish 101

FROM THE VERY FIRST SOUND we make: the birth-cry, to the very last one, the death-cry, and all those in between including the pauses, the silences, looks and gestures, we convey meaning and purpose to those around us and ourselves using language.

I believe that much of our language is attributed to children. While adults teach us how to communicate and the meaning of words and how they should be used, children play an integral role in the development of language. For example, how many of us experienced words that children make up for people, places and things, and how many of those terms stick around as we pass them on from generation to generation?

Language was created so that we can express how we feel and what we feel towards each other. Think about it, there are over 2,000 languages spoken around the world, and I am always curious how these languages came about, have changed over time, the mix and interplay of languages and the people who speak them, the imposition of languages, the corruption or evolution of language (depending on the point of view), and why some of these languages still exist, while others have faded away.

And this process is never-ending, it doesn't stop, nor does it proceed in a vacuum. The natural wanderings of humankind, the forced migrations of people due to change in climate, natural disaster, and even changes of a political or economic nature that bring about an ever-changing interplay where people of different origins, cultures and languages meet.

These are some basic ideas I wanted to share with you that come from my own perspective. Feel free to send me your comments and ideas, including criticisms. ◄

[Feb. 2002]

Spanglish

These words I graft
upon the skin of a white
universe
to give it meaning,
shape, form
and a purpose
for being
using some cosmic
alphabet
to reconstruct
the pan-galactic
mother tongue
SPANGLISH
is a dictionary
of cultural
intercourse
to bridge
all species
of Alien Nation
for here
we say

I am

It is the birth-cry
of another nation
without a flag
or borders
we are all
      the dead
           the living
and the semi-retired
of a cosmic

Alien Nation
far flung
across
TIME, SPACE
and Gravitation

As we gravely
Gravitate
to our
Terminal Destinations
while my pen
scratches
the surface
of this dream
screaming
at the edges
of a borderless nation

I AM!

13.
Nuyorican: A New Language

WHILE THE EXPERTS HAVE BEEN tackling this subject for years, here we are, trying to sort this all out in our attempt to determine what "Nuyorican" means to us.

Here's what I think: The story about language and how we communicate to each other has taken over a millenia to develop. It has mutated, festered and sprung forth from the bad and the good, from wars, slavery, colonization and the killing of civilizations. Our language has been confronted, co-opted and compromised. This is no indictment, it's simply fact.

Because through all of that, we managed to continue to love ourselves and one another; express creatively our highest aspirations; nurture and welcome others; and in some cases, give our lives to save others.

The very urge to communicate and the means by which we do, reflect both the very best and worst in us. Language itself is imposed from within; language and identity become the source of how we communicate with each other. I keep repeating this, but it always come back to how the conquerors used language to impose an "us" versus "them" strategy in order to exclude and differentiate us from one another for political and monetary gain. More importanty, they used langauge to strip our indigenous identities. Of course even today, the imposition of language continues from the written word to visual sound bites we're constantly bombarded with; through education, peer and group pressures; how we communicate amongst ourselves, our families our friends; to how we communicate through cultural, artistic, religious and even scientific exchanges.

Besides exploring the dynamic interaction between different cultural groups and languages, I also want to talk a little bit about identity and how we see ourselves. I also want to investigate how the expression of art arises from such play and how culture, language and people come together.

It's a New World and the "Babel" of nationalities, languages, cultures and identities that have developed for generations will continue to do so for generations to come. Let's bring it home! ◀

[Mar. 2002]

14.
More on Language

IN MY PREVIOUS COMMENTS on the development of language and identity, I've pointed out that this has been a slow, organic, methodical evolution to a more inclusive, yet profound and varied view on how we can learn to understand who we are. The development of language ties into how we identify ourselves as human beings.

What I have neglected to mention is how technology has affected language today, and how it's played an increased role in the development and propagation of new words, slang and jargon. There used to be a time when it would take maybe several generations to develop a new language and new terms; but now we are confronted with new words with new meanings through emails and texting.

Due to technology, the world has become a much smaller place. We're global! We readily and easily communicate with people around the world. And as people come up with new ways to spell words and create new terms, they get passed around almost immediately. Language is no longer bound by neighborhoods, cities, states and countries. Someone can create a new term and in an instance, people all over the world begin using it. This increased turnover of words is the very reason why we should explore these changes and how it relates to art.

We're living in a new world. The "Babel" of nationalities, languages, cultures and identity are merging and coming together.

You too are a Nuyorican. *Welcome Home.* ◀

[Mar. 2002]

15.
Ancestral Native American Language and Traditions: Another Viewpoint

WITH MY APOLOGIES TO THE FIRST PEOPLE for any offense perceived as intended or a result of my incomplete knowledge of their past.

The story below is an excerpt of a narrative from an unpublished manuscript by yours truly that I wrote in 1996, that I would like to share with you.

> Once upon a long (very long) time ago, in a land close at hand, lived a people, the Children of the Word of the Great Spirit in the Sky. And they spoke with all the sounds of Air, Earth, Water and Life. They were fierce, independent, proud, and happy. Their days were long and plentiful, with joyful nights given to the telling of long stories about their origins and the days of the Old Fathers. They also took great pleasure in displaying their creative

talents by imitating all the sounds they heard and creating new ones for each new story. They would repeat the ancient stories, sound by sound from the Old Fathers, and would make new ones to tell at The Gathering.

On the First New Moon, the clans would meet to judge which story would represent them at the next New Moon, to be repeated at each New Moon. At the Second New Moon, the clans of each Tribe would select which Tribal Story would be told at the next New Moon. Then the Tribes of each Nation, would do the same, and the Nations of each Old Father would follow suite. From time to time it varied, depending on how many new nations, tribes and clans were formed as they roamed the land. This tradition went on for many Moons.

There was a time when The Gathering would happen once every couple of generations, but as more time passed between The Gatherings, more new words were being formed. As their speech, customs and way of living became more distinct, it was becoming increasingly difficult for the Tribes to understand each other. Disagreements ensued, animosities ran rampant. Soon, The Gathering was marked by the Star of the Serpent: fights broke out and blood was shed. The Elders of the Gathering met and agreed that for the sake of the Old Fathers, the People could no longer be as One. From that moment going forward, the Tribes would walk on different paths and The Gathering would be no more. They cried and parted with the Hope that one day their descendants would reunite and become One People once again.

Unfortunately, The Gathering never happened and eventually the Children of the Word of the Great Spirit in the Sky and their legacy was obliterated by the passage of time. Remnants of their history can be found in the language we speak today by the names of various regions, landmarks, animals and plants, but The Gathering would be no more.

A People once lived and walked the land between the North and South Poles, who dreamed and danced, who spoke thousands of languages, who constructed marvels and then seemingly disappeared overnight, with few remembering the words of the First People: "Until the Next Gathering."

Language is more than a collection of sounds bound by rules, structure and meaning. It's also rhythm, sequence, sound and vibration that elicit an order and pattern that we perceive and is within the realm of our perceptions.

The "Babel" of nationalities, languages, cultures and identity continues to play an important role in how we speak, and how we identify ourselves as human beings. ◄

You too are a Nuyorican. *Welcome home.*

[Jul. 2002]

16.
Salute to the Nuyoricans

I'VE SPOKEN ABOUT THE GENESIS of the term "Nuyorican" and how it has branched out into multiple meanings. And while there has been a generation of Nuyoricans who have expressed their art through music (the lyrics and the sound), poetry and theater (performed, spoken, read or written), visual art and film, it's interesting to note that the Cafe has had a fantastic group of people who may not consider themselves "Nuyorican," but have subscribed to what Nuyorican is all about. There are just too many to mention, but here are a few that come to mind:

> Héctor LaVoe, Piri Thomas, Miguel Algarin, Pedro Pietri, Lucky Cienfuegos, Miguel Piñero, Caridad de la Luz, Mariposa, Shaggy Flores, Gustavo Escanlar, Adrian Villegas, Eduardo Flores, Felipe Luciano, Felipe Campos, Victor Hernández Cruz, Adal Maldonado, Raul Maldonado, Eddie Figueroa, José Angel Figueroa, Jesús Papoleto Meléndez,

Lois Griffith, Sandra María Esteves, Tito Goya, Rome Neal, Felice Belle, Aileen Reyes, Nathan P., REO III, reg e gaines, Savion Glover, Flaco Navaja, Angelo Lozada, Danny Gonzalez, Nancy Mercado, Anthony Morales, Clare Ultimo, Mayda del Valle, Chris Washbourne, Rocky, Bobby Sanabria, Bimbo Rivas, Tato Laviera.

Some are still here and have become widely known, others you may have never heard of, and sadly, some are no longer with us. I salute them all.

[Sep. 2002]

Bimbo

another voice in the desert is silent
though the wind continues to whisper a
babelian thread weaving the story that
doesn't end at the edge of the desert
this lonely pause seeps deep within
against a backdrop of continuous creation
to mark the ancient question

another moment in the long succession
of words written upon the shifting sands
this space speaks volumes and you can't hear
what this silence withholds, this answer
that never makes sense in whatever language
you choose to listen, carefully upon the wind

another place at the edge of imagination
falls over the event horizon of our perceptions
but never forgotten, these words are etched
in blood, upon the surface of time, have
we left a sign to whom would remember us
in exchange for our not forgetting the wild
stream of thoughts impressed upon our souls
by the never ending poem that eats its own

another grain of sand lifted by the wind
to comply with the ancient entropic directive
that disperses each thought to the edge
of this ever-increasing desert, running
at the speed of light, never catching up
with a past that never stays the same
of a future that never gets here, compelling
us to continually search the hidden
places in our minds, for a reason or

any excuse why is it a voice is silenced
but the poem goes on oblivious, indifferent
to the bloody tracks we leave behind

another question goes unanswered
and we thrash against the confines
of this terminal abode that bids we settle down
to an eternal wait for the long awaited answer
that never comes within listening distance
as if six feet under were so far away
or long ago, we could not understand
in whatever tongue it chose to remain silent
as we grieve with the certainty that
for all the questions we scream
in the middle of this lonesome night
we know there is no answer to this silence.

Ragged Edge

There's a ragged edge
to the whisper
of the wind tonight
you hear the news
of all your fears
mark the passage
of another race
to the end
of a story
before time runs
out of here
and winds up
to the point
of no return
though you must know
you can't go back
still you try
just in case
you get a second chance
before you hear an echo
of a rumbling sigh
Judgment Day approaches
and you can't remember
what you've done
to make appropriate excuses
or a reasonable alibi
the hour creaks slowly
time groans under the weight
of all that matters
this late in the song
to another time
lost in space

and all the stars
from the sky
dare not interfere
with a dream about to end
silent, awed and respectful
witnesses all
to another poem or song
to add to the long parade
but tonight my friend
give pause to your deeds
for the wind tonight
has a ragged edge

17.
Spanish: Romancing the Nuyorican

A LANGUAGE DOES NOT EVOLVE into another language in a vacuum, nor does it arrive fully formed. It evolves over space and time, and its development is neither linear nor logical. Spanish is such a language. In fact, I've read and studied up on this a bit and learned that our "Spanglish" comes from Latin (okay, by way of Spanish, or as we like to refer to it as "Puerto Rican Spanish").

As with most languages, Latin became a language out of necessity to govern empires. In time, a group of languages often referred to as "Romance languages" descended from Latin. The five most widely spoken Romance languages by number of native speakers are Spanish, Portuguese, French, Italian, and believe it or not, Romanian.

Spanish is derived from a dialect of spoken Latin that evolved in the north-central part of the Iberian Peninsula after the fall of the Western Roman Empire in the fifth century. In about a thousand years, the language would eventually expand south to the Mediterranean Sea, and would later be taken up in the Spanish colonial empire, most notably, the Americas. As Spain expanded its empire, the Spanish language was imposed to maintain political, economic and even religious control of the population. But in its quest, the conquistadors were unable to totally eradicate the local languages, and over time the people would adapt by adopting the local flavor of their language into Spanish, which is how we speak Spanish today. (By the way, the Spanish we speak today has lexical borrowings from the indigenous languages of the Americas, like for us Puerto Ricans, *Taíno*.) That's why Spanish-speaking people from different parts of the world have their own lingo. That's why, for example, while Puerto Ricans, Dominicans and Mexicans speak Spanish, they use different words or phrases that come from their respective indigenous cultures.

It should be noted that the local language in the Iberian lands were being increasingly influenced by the language of the Moors (Arab population). This influence persisted for many centuries and eventually became part of the standard Spanish (Castilian), which is spoken today. Although treated lightly by the history books, the interplay of these two unrelated languages greatly affected the Spanish language, even the identity of the people. So while The Royal Spanish Academy (the official royal institution responsible for overseeing how the Spanish language should be spoken) continues to hassle us over the "proper" way to speak Spanish, it's us indigenous folks who have enforced and preserved the development of a language that truly reflects our culture and who we are. To further emphasize my point, here's where the poet, writer, artist, and performer come in: by creating art in their communities and taking the language of the streets, the language became universal as it became a part of us.

I want to continue investigating our linguistic background through art and what poets and artists are doing with language as it relates to the Nuyorican Arts Movement. Take time to take a closer look at poetry and ask yourself this: Why do we seek to express ourselves with words, and how does art reflect the language we speak?

[Sep. 2002]

18.
Poetic Aside: Amiri Baraka

Thou Shall Not Silence The Poet

It is with deep concern, grave misgivings and a rising state of apprehension that I have been reading about and have been made aware of a dark, sinister, destructive and evil conspiracy against the Word, Poetry and the Poet, being implemented by the Forces of Darkness against the Light and Creation.

And while I, Poet, normally would hold my peace and let others do as they will, I will not be silent in the face of Evil being perpetrated in the Name of Peace, the Greater Good or even Planetary Security. To remain silent, in this case would be to consent, to agree. I DO NOT.

Thou Shall Not Silence The Poet

If you don't like what you hear, you don't have to listen. "Seek and you shall find," and "the truth shall set you free"

If you don't like the Poet, you do not have to listen. Be a better

Poet.

If you don't like the Poem. Be on the side of Creation, make a better one, not on the side of destruction to erase it.

And while I, Poet, will not tell you what to do, say, or believe, just so that you will know:

> Life creates,
> While, Death eats its own.
> You can stop a poem
> You cannot stop THE WORD!

Thou Shall Not Silence The Poet

And while I may differ (as all poets do from each other) in the voice, ethnicity, religious belief, socio-economic status, political affiliations, cultural background, family traditions, genetic composition, blood type, language, rhythm, cadence, personal preferences, philosophical beliefs, I, Poet, shall not remain silent and will always stand on the side of the creative expression of the WORD. You are either for Creation or against Creation.

Thou Shall Not Silence The Poet

A Poet true to his profession, true to his art, true to the Word requires no accolade, honor or title. But if such is given by others, to then silence the Poet is an indictment of those who gave the accolade, the honor or the title. Their loss, their shame.

I, Sam Diaz, Poet, salute Amiri Baraka, Poet.

> "Thou Shall Not Silence The Poet"
> "Thou Shall Not Silence The Poet"
> "Thou Shall Not Silence Amiri Baraka" ◄

[Nov. 2002]

19.
Poetic Aside: "Bienal de la Poesia"

I BEGAN WRITING THESE NOTES on my way to "Muestra de la Poesia Nacional" sponsored by "Bienal de la Poesia" in Puerto Rico towards the end of October. Bienal de la Poesia is an organization of poets, writers, artists and members of various artistic groups, including graphic artist, promoters, professors under the direction of Lcdo. Luis Antonio Rosario Quiles. The group calls itself Concilio, but I translate it as a Congress of Poets. It selects Poets to be honored on the basis of published work, referrals by fellow poets and interviews with the group, after which a Nomination is given. Located in Puerto Rico and dedicated to recognizing and promoting Puerto Rican poets and poetry (established and emerging), it sponsors events at various locations. Their main event was held at "Museo de Arte de Puerto Rico," San Juan, Puerto Rico, October 26, 2002.

[*Correction:* This event was known as "the Ante-sala" or Preview of the actual Bienal de la Poesia, which was held in March 2003, and which I also attended]

Twenty-two Poets, selected by Bienal as representatives from the 1960s and 1970s generation of writers, participated. Nineteen read in person, the others through prerecorded submissions. They represented a wide sampling of styles, thematic and structural, but it was straight poetry throughout, without the stage props, performances, dedications and or even introductory words. A name is given, a sampling of poems to background music provided by Eddie Figueroa, then applause, pause and next. It was a joy to see so many poets that I have long admired, some that I have known personally for more years than we care to admit, and some that were somewhat known (by their fame), with a couple of surprises, all in a syncopated, structured flow of poetry that left us all stunned and awed. It was over too soon, but right on time to a roar of approval. And that was a "Muestra" or Sample.

And included in that list of poets was the Reverend Pedro Pietri, a Boricua, a Puerto Rican, a Nuyorican, as part of the National Poetry. As it should be. Twenty-one poets read in Spanish, Pedro read in English. There was a reflex gasp, he read, and then a standing ovation from the audience that told him (and us), "you are part of us." As it should be.

Then there was another poetry event, some from the Bienal, some local, and Nuyoricans at The Nuyorican Cafe in Old San Juan (no affiliation). What a treat! They were very friendly host. The staff was great, the space was nice and we listened to some good poetry. Mariposa was in town, sharing her performance with all of us. As we were leaving, our host, Juanra Gwen introduced himself to us, asking us to keep in touch, and to establish closer ties with the two Cafes, which we will.

While all this was enjoyable, it was the prospect of continued collaboration between the different groups, poets, and friends that made the event even more memorable.

The Muestra will be held every other year, as will the Bienal festivities. If I understood correctly, la Muestra emphasizes the Poets of a particular generation. The next generation to be honored will be the 1980s. The Bienal events honor poetry as a National Legacy. The next Bienal will be held in Puerto Rico, starting March 1, 2003 (International Poetry Day) and ending sometime after March 21st. And The Nuyorican Poets Cafe will be participating at different levels with the Bienal, once all the necessary agreements are in place. One of our possible roles would be to act as a conduit for identifying Poets in the U.S. who should be considered part of the Puerto Rican Poetic Legacy. In addition, we might sponsor poets who are directly affiliated with the Cafe to represent a "Nuyorican" delegation to events in Puerto Rico. There's also the possibility of organizing contacts for groups in New York that wish to participate under their own auspices. Other ideas that are being discussed include sponsoring "Bienal" and "Muestra" events in the mainland, and providing venues for the Poets on tour.

It was hard to leave all the poetry and friends behind, but the prospect of a continuing poetic dialogue makes it easier to look forward to next year, while at the same time the memory of all this poetry and friendship, makes me say "Thanks!" ◀

[Jan. 2003]

Don't Ask, I Won't Tell You

Don't ask me
what am I
I am not a what
but a who I am
If you wish to know
Though I probably
won't tell you
anyway

Be careful
what you ask
and of whom you ask
when you believe
in the labels
of your choice
even though
they may not be
what you think
they are

For though labels
we must use
do not confuse
the label with
what it describes
which is always
more than
labels can define

And I know
you mean no harm
and then again
what do I know
if you know

what I mean
but it seems to me
you have much
to learn or fear
from the
likes of me
when you deny
who I am
for the what
I might be

And if it's not
easy to guess
then I guess
You will ask
what you must
And I will answer
as I will

And though
You'll be wrong
in either case
I may reply
or maybe not
in either case
it may be so
and then maybe not
you may hear
what you please
or not
either for
who I am
or what you
think I am
but never
what am I

Poetry Never Dies

And if I
should silent fall
weep not for me
but for the silence about

Poetry never dies

As I lay claim
to the unbroken legacy
of words upon the wind
to proclaim for all to hear

Poetry never dies

And even dead
I know I have won
the battle against entropy
and orders imposed

Poetry never dies

And in the eternal
succession of words
silent I will not remain
another poet will be born

Poetry never dies

And long after the end of time
the word continues
just because it goes on

Poetry never dies

And if all of us
should cease to exist
somewhere in the universe
words will be heard

Poetry never dies

and in a strange tongue
will I hear
from 6 feet under
and in my dreams

Poetry never dies

I Poet salute
another silent voice
another silent poet
for the universe to know

Poetry never dies

Invisible Poem

It's an invisible poem
At the edge
Of a disappearing desert
All eyes on you
As you catch your next breath

I close my eyes
You see me not

Single file we walk
Oblivious to the sights
We see and
The sounds we make
As we mutter 'scuse me
While I die

I close my eyes
You see me not

Careful to mind
My p's and q's
Dot my I's and cross my t's
Mindful of labels
And the words I use not
For fear
You'll hate me
Or think
I hate you

I close my eyes
You see me not

As I wounded walk
In borrowed pain
As if I had none
To call my own
You take my principal
And you tax my interest
But I remain in debt
Eternal compound
Loops back to you
With no exemptions
To deduct from
A sentence without end

I close my eyes
You see me not

20.
Poetic Aside: Slam News/Poetry on Broadway and a Happy New Year!

Nuyorican New Year's Resolution:
1. I resolve to not make any resolutions that I cannot keep! (oops!)

So much for good intentions. A new year does not necessarily mean a fresh start or a clean slate. That's a calendar thing. You still carry the leftovers from the day before and get to add some more. But the mark on the calendar is still appropriate as a gentle reminder of the past. I started writing these comments in the afterglow of holiday festivities, family gatherings and some very poetic events. I could not help but notice a sadness lingering while all of this was going on. Family, friends and poets, no longer with us. The ones we would love to share those moments with when we celebrate the ties that bind us together. So a new year starts by looking back, and perhaps therein may lay new things to come.

The last Slam of the Year was also Felice Belle's last Slam as our Slam Director. It was an evening of poetry at its best. (For reviews and notices, check out the Poetry/Slam pages.) The best of the best paid poetic homage to Felice that left many of us wondering why we don't do this kind of event on a regular basis. Yes, I know the night was special and it was for Felice after all, but it still left us wanting more. As Felice goes on to new endeavors, she will always remain a part of us, as a new Slam Director, Karen Jaime, comes on board to continue this Nuyorican tradition.

The Nuyorican Slam has become an important part of our tradition. Every year as new talent comes through the Cafe, many wind-up representing the Cafe at the National Slams, and then they move on and a new team takes their place. Over the years, we've developed a long roster of the best that Slam or competitive performance poetry has to offer. Win, lose or draw, poetry wins. And yes, I got to see a good representation of our slammers on Broadway!!! Yep, I did get to see *Def Poetry Jam* on Broadway. Who woulda thought?!?

Okay, what follows is not a review, nor a critique. I am a poet, but as an entertainer (or performer), I would never make it in that venue. So I am usually impressed by just about any performance and in this case, I was awestruck. And it hurts, 'cause I can't do it!

The poets and the poetry were great. Since I know most of them, have seen them perform and know their work, some of them on *Def Poetry Jam* on HBO, I've had some expectations of what I would see. And I must confess, the Broadway show was better than I ever expected, by a long shot.

But —

My personal preferences on poetry have always been, the Poem and the Poet. As our Sage Seer from A Gathering of the Tribes, Steve Cannon, would say: "The poem, read the poem!" I wanted to hear more poetry, more poems, more poets. But this is Broadway. It's a show.

And herein lies the difference one does not encounter at poetry readings. A poet reads and the body of the work they presents is tied into them. But in a stage production, there has to be a thread, a cohesive story. How do you manage that? How do you take the words of so many different voices, styles and individual perspectives and create a cohesive story? Mission impossible? If it is, then I have to admit that the show comes as close to it as possible. And you, lovers of poetry, should see it.

But —

And here I go, once again, expressing my own personal preferences. I prefer the one on one and, give and take of a poet, reading or performing their work.

I wanted to hear more Mayda Del Valle (she's become one of my favorites, it's a Nuyorican Thing!, OK?), More Suheir!, More Black Ice! More, more and more from each and every one of these great poets. Even the shared poems and poetic dialogues were great.

But —

There is a thin line that separates collective poetry from poetry by committee. Aside from some brief points of clarity, I think the group as a whole could have been better choreographed. Yes, I do understand that the many voices of poetry can be perceived as a cacophonous "Babel of Poets" speaking in tongues. Yes, I do understand the difficulty encountered by the show's producers in trying to keep it real and at the same time tell a story (a la Broadway). And in a real sense, the show simply reflects reality.

So, from the bottom of my heart, and in the name of Poetry, I thank you for attempting the impossible and for bringing the word to thirsty ears. Poetry on Broadway! Who woulda thought!?!◄

[Feb. 2003, web]

21.
Art and Community

AT THE BOTTOM OF THE PAGE you see my signoff: "In the Service of Poetry, Art and Community." The reason why I say this is because I believe that poetry and art are not only important ways for people to express themselves creatively, it is the responsibility of the poet and the artist to connect with each other as a unified community. So for the sake of these comments, think of community as: "Unity in common, or common unity," a bonding between members of a group based on its relationship to the arts. Sounds simple, but it's not. For as much as language and identity are open-ended concepts, community also requires a claim, a recognition, an acceptance, and therein lies the complexity.

For many centuries, poetry movements and communities have served as the most provocative, creative, vital, engaging, and oft-underground elements of regional and national literary trends. The simple joy of gathering for a poetry reading, listening to verse, hearing background stories, and discussing poetry has joined and empowered poets from ancient Athens to the streets of New York City. These assemblies have launched social and political discourse, like the creation of the Nuyorican movement, while feeding creative explosions that, in nearly all cases, involved the arts.

We are a part of many communities, as much as they are part of us. Some communities are defined by location, cultural, political or of a vocational persuasion. But it's also true that just claiming to be a member of a particular community doesn't automatically make you a part of the community. Too many people claim membership but do nothing to help sustain their community. As poets and artists, it is incumbent upon us to do just that.

The Nuyorican Poets Cafe is a community of poets and artists that over the years has expanded beyond its initial ethnic connotation, to a more universal inclusiveness. While its artistic avocation continues to be the common unifying bond, the Cafe is constantly expanding its membership in a number of communities. As a collective, the Cafe is a member of the Lower East Side community. It's a member of various city, state, national and international Arts communities. It is part of the Latino/Hispanic/ Puerto Rican communities. And it is part of the Federation of East Village Artists Community, a vocation community. The Cafe has taken great pride in participating in the first annual HOWL! Festival of East Village Arts, sponsored by FEVA and HOWL (www. howlfestival.com). We will give more details later on this, but I mention it here to emphasize the community aspect of it.

As a stand-alone art form, poetry is and has always been the least lucrative form of writing. Regardless of the promotional and distribution venues available, the business of poetry remains now as it has for three millenia—very hard work that earns very little money. Yet, poets have never written poems to make money. They write poems because something deep inside calls for expression, and they know there is only one thing to do—express it. Over the years they have worked as a community to make change, to make things happen. It just seems that nowadays, we've lost sight of what community is all about. We're so busy getting wrapped up into the business of poetry and the arts, some of us have forgotten why we got into in the first place. I am hoping that we will get back to that soon, because the world has become a different place. We need to become more attuned to our communities; it's the only way we will truly survive. It's also my sincere hope that perhaps one day we will extend our community to all the other communities on planet Earth. Maybe then we will find peace.

In the Service of Poetry, Art and Community. ◄

[Jun. 2003]

22.
Who Owns Art?

I PUT THESE COMMENTS finally to the page in the aftermath of a very stressful season (being of a tropical persuasion, I prefer to think of it as the eye of the storm). While it's true that these circumstances are personal, they may have some bearing on the theme at hand.

When we create art, we often must isolate ourselves from the very same people we wish to share it with. I have a friend, a well-known poet undergoing stressful times. He was, until a couple of days ago, staying here with us. One of the things he's had to deal with is the inability to write with an ease that's always come natural to him. Having to endure a number of physical ailments, this hurt him the most, making his isolation almost unbearable.

This isolation is perhaps a requirement for most creative endeavors. For some creative souls it's part of their psyche, while for others creative isolation is contrary to their nature. But when one is immersed in creating their work, sometimes something comes out of nothing and we're so happy with the progress we've made, we want to share it with others. It's food for the soul. My friend managed to write some poems in the middle of his madness, and the first thing he did was share them with his friends. Poetry never gives up.

It's the very nature of writing where the concept of ownership becomes troublesome. The writer uses words that belong to no one. No one owns language. Not even the people who speak it, or the established agencies that determine its proper use. Even words that have been made up and used in a work of art, wind up being owned by no one. As terms, phrases and words become widely incorporated into language, even the writer who created it is going to have a hard time claiming ownership.

When my friend writes poetry, he inks reams of paper. When I typed some of his work, the spellcheck goes crazy because every other word is not found in the dictionary. Was the word misspelled, or did he create a new word? And of course, when he writes in "Spanglish" we tell the computer to shut up. That is the beauty behind creating poetry. It makes the isolation, the desire to contemplate in quietness worth it.

Well, this is some of my random thoughts on this odd vocation that has chosen us, Poetry. Write, we must. In doing so, we explore who we are in the process and then share our collection of words to the world, hoping to find a home in the heart of the reader. Let's further explore this labor of love in our next "Our Nuyorican Thing."

> [My friend has left on a journey for the fight of a lifetime. Have no doubt, Poetry never gives up!]◄

[Jan. 2004]

23.
Time after Time

WHEN WRITING THESE COMMENTARIES in "Our Nuyorican Thing" I was reminded that the series was never meant to flow or read as a book. It was always intended as sporadic commentaries about poetry, art and the "Nuyorican" phenomena. So I will continue to remain true to this cause, and who knows, perhaps one day these commentaries will find themselves on the printed page.

It's interesting to note that "Our Nuyorican Thing" began because people were interested in exploring the meaning behind Nuyorican and the dilemma of identity. Despite the progress we've made over the years, we still grapple with who we are individually and collectively as a group. Do we accept this term, or do we refuse it? Or does it refuse us?

It seems that identity is not an easy thing to tackle. As human beings, each of us is unique and different, yet we long to belong to a community. I'm willing to continue on this journey, are you? Let me know what you think. ◄

[Feb. 2004]

24.
What Silence Says About Art

THE SHORT GLIB TECHNICAL ANSWER would be: Nothing! But silence is a necessary and integral part of communication. The poet, writer, painter, musician and all artists use all of their skills to express their perception and understanding of life. But sometimes "Silence" is its own communication. Not just the silent pause between verses or notes, but the more emphatic: Stop. Not the "stop" at the end of a poem, or musical composition, or an art object, but a silence that elicits a response, a silence that questions, a silence that manages to overwhelm the soul.

The Poet is Silent.
>   So that communication may continue, as in dialogic (or multilogic, as the case may be).
>   So that Art may be more than just an imitation of Life,
>   So as to allow space for the next step (Poem, Poet, Artistic expression).
>   So as to understand when life is also Silent.

The Poet is Silent

So as to gather thought, understanding and inspiration.
So as to weigh the significance (or lack thereof), of what has been created.
So as to share, show, or give (or destroy, sometimes) what Art has done.
So as to allow time to heal the wounds of work done.

And while, for the most part, artistic dialogue is avidly sought (to varying degrees), sometimes it's the silence that is necessary and much appreciated. It's also true that poets will continue to create and make noise whether its approved or not, or even when there is no response, until the final silence, even after their "Silent Terminal Stop."

We will continue the comments on ownership of Art, at a later time, but consider the issue, not just from the perspective of the Poet, or the perceiver (observer), but also the arbiter who labels and/or defines it. ◀

[May 2004]

Silent Poem

I've few words
to share today
not for lack
or reasons none

but today I share
what silence may say
when words can not
say what we must

what words will I say
that will still
the pain I see
or which we can't

tell me a word
to fill the hunger
of a child
a tearless sigh
away from death

so today I share
what silence will do
when words will not
do what we must

give me a word
to heal the sick
in death's grip
before there's
naught to be done

tell me the word
to soothe the rage
we must have
of the innocent
put to death

today I must share
a silent pause
from too many words

New Millennium Poets

I once was young
but now I'm not
was full of rage and fury
and howled into the night
I burnt paper and cloth
and refused to move on

I once was young
but now I'm not
was full of words and poetry
and didn't go to sleep
unless it was to nod

I once was young
but now I'm not
was full of love, justice & music
and sung out loud at the march

I once was young
but now I'm not
was full of righteous indignation
at the sight of injustice
bigotry and discrimination
and spoke to crowds
in a low slow rage
and heard them roar

I once was young
but now I'm not
about a minute ago.

So now I come
to places like this

to hear new
young angry poets
not let me forget
to remind me
this war goes on
but before I go
to join the long
slow parade
these words
with you I leave

Rave On
never stop
Rage on
never shut up

Rage at all
the evil you see
and whatever
wrong you hear
and from a blank page
left, right,
center or no stage

RAGE, RAGE, RAGE
against evil, hate
lies and death
against the day
that would be night
against the wrong
that would be right
against whatever
makes you rage

Rave On
never stop
Rage on
never shut up

And when your voice
gives out on you
and your vision
is blurred
and your words
are slurred
and dreams
turn to wishes
and all you energies
are spent,
stop by a place
such as this
where young
angry poets rage
to remember
to recharge
and tell them
for me
and all the voices
at the edge of a blank page

Rave On
never stop
Rage on
never shut up
Rave On
never stop
Rage on
never shut up

The Long Goodbye

Add another sold
to the long good bye
as you freely barter
for another day
as we pay
with interest
all our deeds done

Add another tear
to the endless sea of love
as you remember
a passing sigh
proper verification
for you are still alive

Add another step
to the long parade
that pauses so often
to mark the place
I last saw you

Add another sigh
to our held breath
now out of view
to measure the distance
from the memory
of your existence
in our last walk
together
down memory lane

Add another stone
to the forever hereafter
I remember you path
that leads us
all back home
in the buy and bye
when we meet again

AFTER :: WORDS

THERE WERE OTHER ESSAYS FROM "Our Nuyorican Thing" that were not included in this collection, namely, commentaries written by other people, such as a poetic tribute to the Nuyorican Poets Cafe by Joe Ubiles. What's included here is a selection of my essays which I hope presents a wide range of ideas as it pertains to The Nuyorican Poets Cafe and the mission I undertook when writing for "Our Nuyorican Thing" and an exploration of Nuyorican identity. I also included poetry that I read at the Cafe during this period as well.

The final essay, "What Silence Says About Art" proved to be a longer pause then planned as I took on additional responsibilities at the Cafe. At the time, the essay was meant as a break from writing while I organized my thoughts to address the very complex issue of ownership of art in "Who Owns Art" published January 2004. My friend the Poet continued on his journey, to places beyond our "ken" (nice old Scottish term), leaving an amazing legacy of poetry and art. Once I wrote "What Silence Says About Art," the pause became a stop. And the stop became silence.

For some time I have been considering the idea of ownership as much as death. Death seems so final, but life continues on. The Poet dies, and poetry goes on, but the work he creates belongs to him, no matter what.

Which brings me to the point where I get to quote myself:

"From my mouth to your ears
it now belongs to the air"

As a poet I lay claim to my poems. I use words that existed long before I did to create prose and poems, using a name that was given to me by my parents and forbearers (that has been officially accepted by the proper civilian authorities), which are signed by me (with writing implement made by someone else), to attest to the fact that I am who I claim to be.

On the one hand (with my apologies to the other), I do so with the air that we breathe and speak to convey words of my own choosing.

And of course, with an other hand (with my apologies to the other), I have the audacity to request compensation from you, dear reader, so you can read my stuff!!! And the clincher: It's still mine after I die!!!

But does all of this really answer the question: Who Owns Art? You decide. ◄

—Samuel Diaz Carron
In the Service of Poetry, Art and Community

[2013]

PHOTO: Vagabond

ABOUT THE AUTHOR

SAMUEL DIAZ CARRON is a Puerto Rican poet and writer born in the South Bronx. While working as a chemist, he participated in meetings that led to he founding of the Nuyorican Poets Café, New Rican Village and other venues. Over the years, he has coordinated poetry and reading series, and managed theatrical events for Pedro Pietri and the Nuyorican Poets Café.

Diaz also served as a coordinator for the Puerto Rican-based Bienal de la Poesía Puertorriqueña and subsequent events for La Muestra de la Bienal. He established Bronx Computerized Administrative Office Services (BxCAOS) to assist small business personal companies and not for profit organizations in the community and arts fields. He provided services to the Nuyorican Poets Cafe starting in 1996, and worked as an information services assistant, bookkeeper and then Office Director until he retired in 2006. ◄

OTHER BOOKS BY 2LEAF PRESS

2LEAF PRESS challenges the status quo by publishing alternative fiction, non-fiction, poetry and bilingual works by activists, academics, poets and authors dedicated to diversity and social justice with scholarship that is accessible to the general public. 2LEAF PRESS produces high quality and beautifully produced hardcover, paperback and ebook formats through our series: *2LP Explorations in Diversity, 2LP University Books, 2LP Classics, 2LP Translations, Nuyorican World Series,* and *2LP Current Affairs, Culture & Politics.* Below is a selection of 2LEAF PRESS' published titles.

2LP EXPLORATIONS IN DIVERSITY
Substance of Fire: Gender and Race in the College Classroom
by Claire Millikin
Foreword by R. Joseph Rodríguez, Afterword by Richard Delgado
Contributed material by Riley Blanks, Blake Calhoun, Rox Trujillo

Black Lives Have Always Mattered
A Collection of Essays, Poems, and Personal Narratives
Edited by Abiodun Oyewole

The Beiging of America:
Personal Narratives about Being Mixed Race in the 21st Century
Edited by Cathy J. Schlund-Vials, Sean Frederick Forbes, Tara Betts
with an Afterword by Heidi Durrow

What Does it Mean to be White in America?
Breaking the White Code of Silence, A Collection of Personal Narratives
Edited by Gabrielle David and Sean Frederick Forbes
Introduction by Debby Irving and Afterword by Tara Betts

2LP UNIVERSITY BOOKS
Designs of Blackness, Mappings in the Literature and
Culture of African Americans
A. Robert Lee
20TH ANNIVERSARY EXPANDED EDITION

2LP CLASSICS
Adventures in Black and White
Edited and with a critical introduction by Tara Betts
by Philippa Duke Schuyler

Monsters: Mary Shelley's Frankenstein and Mathilda
by Mary Shelley, edited by Claire Millikin Raymond

2LP TRANSLATIONS
Birds on the Kiswar Tree
by Odi Gonzales, Translated by Lynn Levin
Bilingual: English/Spanish

Incessant Beauty, A Bilingual Anthology
by Ana Rossetti, Edited and Translated by Carmela Ferradáns
Bilingual: English/Spanish

NUYORICAN WORLD SERIES
Our Nuyorican Thing, The Birth of a Self-Made Identity
by Samuel Carrion Diaz, with an Introduction by Urayoán Noel
Bilingual: English/Spanish

Hey Yo! Yo Soy!, 40 Years of Nuyorican Street Poetry,
The Collected Works of Jesús Papoleto Meléndez
Bilingual: English/Spanish

LITERARY NONFICTION
No Vacancy; Homeless Women in Paradise
by Michael Reid

The Beauty of Being, A Collection of Fables, Short Stories & Essays
by Abiodun Oyewole

WHEREABOUTS: Stepping Out of Place,
An Outside in Literary & Travel Magazine Anthology
Edited by Brandi Dawn Henderson

PLAYS
Rivers of Women, The Play
by Shirley Bradley LeFlore, with photographs by Michael J. Bracey

AUTOBIOGRAPHIES/MEMOIRS/BIOGRAPHIES
Trailblazers, Black Women Who Helped Make America Great
American Firsts/American Icons
by Gabrielle David

Mother of Orphans
The True and Curious Story of Irish Alice, A Colored Man's Widow
by Dedria Humphries Barker

Strength of Soul
by Naomi Raquel Enright

Dream of the Water Children:
Memory and Mourning in the Black Pacific
by Fredrick D. Kakinami Cloyd
Foreword by Velina Hasu Houston, Introduction by Gerald Horne
Edited by Karen Chau

The Fourth Moment: Journeys from the Known to the Unknown, A Memoir
by Carole J. Garrison, Introduction by Sarah Willis

POETRY
PAPOLíTICO, Poems of a Political Persuasion
by Jesús Papoleto Meléndez
with an Introduction by Joel Kovel and DeeDee Halleck

Critics of Mystery Marvel, Collected Poems
by Youssef Alaoui, with an Introduction by Laila Halaby

shrimp
by jason vasser-elong, with an Introduction by Michael Castro
The Revlon Slough, New and Selected Poems
by Ray DiZazzo, with an Introduction by Claire Millikin

Written Eye: Visuals/Verse
by A. Robert Lee

A Country Without Borders: Poems and Stories of Kashmir
by Lalita Pandit Hogan, with an Introduction by Frederick Luis Aldama

Branches of the Tree of Life
The Collected Poems of Abiodun Oyewole 1969-2013
by Abiodun Oyewole, edited by Gabrielle David
with an Introduction by Betty J. Dopson

2Leaf Press is an imprint owned and operated by the Intercultural Alliance of Artists & Scholars, Inc. (IAAS), a NY-based nonprofit organization that publishes and promotes multicultural literature.

NEW YORK
www.2leafpress.org